Creative Groups Guide

A Call to Prayer

7
**Complete
Lessons**

Adapted for Group Study by Jan Johnson

**STANDARD
PUBLISHING**
Cincinnati, Ohio

Creative Groups Guide: A Call to Prayer

All Scripture quotations, unless otherwise indicated, are taken from the *Holy Bible: New International Version®*, NIV®. Copyright © 1973, 1978, 1984 by International Bible Society. Used by permission of Zondervan Publishing House. All rights reserved.

Scripture quotations marked NASB are taken from The New American Standard Bible, © 1960, 1962, 1968, 1971, 1972, 1973, 1975, 1977 by the Lockman Foundation. Used by permission.

Cover design by SchultzWard, Inc.

The Standard Publishing Company, Cincinnati, Ohio.
A division of Standex International Corporation.

02 01 00 99 98 97 96 95   5 4 3 2 1

ISBN 0-7847-0309-4

Contents

oreword

A Call to Prayer is a challenge to become people of prayer. This call for Christians to pray had a simple beginning. A group discussing how to plant churches and grow them came to this conclusion: "Let's pray and let's encourage others to pray with us, and God will direct his church."

Can we unite in prayer? Think of what could happen—churches setting aside additional time for prayer, Bible colleges uniting in a day of prayer, missionaries praying for their home church, leaders praying for vision, and everyone praying for renewed awareness of church planting, church growth, and teaching. Who knows what the Holy Spirit can yet accomplish through his people?

Awakening! This is what can happen if we will pray.

Will you covenant to pray? Will you covenant to use your influence and level of responsibility in our Lord's church to urge and encourage people to pray? Would you ask others to join you in this covenant?

Jesus said, "Ask the Lord of the harvest . . . to send out workers" (Luke 10:2). What a promise!

Ready to accept the challenge? The challenge is to pray with power and passion about the great biblical themes of revival and of world evangelization.

Many people desire to pray but feel they lack the practical knowledge to be true men and women of prayer. My prayer is that this guide will give the kind of practical help you need to become—and help each of the members of your class or small group to become—a prayer warrior, one whom God can use to change this world.

—David Butts, Compiler of *A Call to Prayer*

Introduction

Welcome to Creative Groups Guides!

Whether your group meets in a classroom at the church building or in the family room in someone's home, this guide will help you get the most out of your session.

You can use this Creative Groups Guide with or without *A Call to Prayer,* the companion book written by eight Christian leaders. Use this guide even if you haven't read that book. But if you do read it, you'll be even more equipped for leading the group.

Each section in this guide includes two plans—one for classes and one for small groups. This gives the leader several options:

- Use the plan just as it is written. If you teach an adult Sunday school or an elective class, use Plan One. If you lead a small group, use Plan Two.

- Perhaps you teach a Sunday school class that prefers a small group style of teaching. Use the discussion questions and activities in Plan Two, but don't overlook the great ideas presented in Plan One. Mix and match the two plans to suit your class.

- Use the best of both plans. Perhaps you could start off your class with a discussion activity in Plan Two, and then use the Bible-study section in Plan One. Use the accountability, worship, or memory verse options presented in Plan Two in your Sunday school class. Use some of the "Sunday school" activities and resource sheets presented in Plan One in your small group meeting. Variety is the spice of life!

Resource sheets in each session are available for you to tear out and photocopy for your class or group. Overhead transparency masters are also included for most sessions. Use your own creativity as you decide how to make these resources work for you.

This guide is meant to help you do several things. First, you'll be able to *facilitate active and interactive learning.* These methods help students remember and put into practice what they learn. Second, you'll *help your class or group apply the lessons to their lives.* These sessions will help your group members actually do something with what they're studying. Third, we've given you *lots of options.* Only you know what will work best in your class or group. Finally, *support and encouragement* are integrated into each session. Learning and application happen best when participants are helping one another. That may mean accountability if your

"Preparing a lesson requires that we as teachers care about what helps people learn. The maxim "The teacher hasn't taught until the learner has learned" insists that we do whatever it takes to challenge participants to understand God's Word and to change their attitudes or behavior to conform with it."

—Jan Johnson, "Prepare for Change: How to Create a Life-Changing Lesson Plan," *Discipleship Journal,* July/August 1994

group has built up the trust and caring it takes, or it may simply mean that people are lovingly encouraging one another to continue growing in knowledge and action.

How to Use This Guide

Each session begins with an excerpt from *A Call to Prayer*. This excerpt summarizes the session at a glance. Use it in your preparation or read it to your class or group as an introduction to a session. The central theme and lesson aims help you understand the main ideas being presented and what outcomes you are looking for.

Materials you might need on hand to conduct your session are listed on the first page of each of the plans.

In both plans, there are three main parts to each session: *Building Community,* a warm-up activity or icebreaker question; *Considering Scripture,* Bible-study activities and discussion; and *Taking the Next Step,* activities or discussion that will help participants apply what they have learned.

In Plan One for Classes, the names of activities are listed in the margins, along with the suggested time for each one. Use these as you plan your lesson and as you teach to stay on track. In most cases, optional activities are listed. Use these instead of or in addition to other activities as time allows.

A number of options are included in Plan Two for groups. Use the accountability-partner option to help the group support, encourage, and hold one another accountable. This works particularly well in a group in which trust has already been gained between participants. Accountability partners can help one another put what they are learning each week into practice. They can pray with and for each other throughout the week. They can "spur one another on toward love and good deeds" (Hebrews 10:24).

Other options include worship ideas and a memory verse. Use these at your discretion to help your group grow in love, devotion, and praise for God and for hiding his Word in their hearts.

Use this guide to help you prepare, but we suggest that you do not take this book to your class or group meeting and merely read from it. Instead, take notes on a separate sheet of paper and use that as you lead your group.

One more thing. If you really want your class or group to grow in their prayer lives, if you want them to come out of this course with a deeper vision for the power of prayer, if you want them to become pray-ers and not just talkers about prayer—then your preparation must include prayer. *Remember to pray for each of the people in your group. Pray for their needs and that their relationship with God will grow through this series.*

One

The Power of Prayer

*M*any of us have been taught that the only reason we pray is to change ourselves. But the Bible does not teach that as a reason to pray. Instead the Bible teaches that prayer affects God and that prayer . . . can affect circumstances. Aren't you affected when your kids talk with you? . . . [God] is the perfect parent as well as the powerful creator. . . .

Some people suggest that God never changes his mind, but listen to what God says about himself . . . "If at any time I announce that a nation or kingdom is to be uprooted, torn down and destroyed, and if that nation I warned repents of its evil, then I will relent and not inflict on it the disaster I had planned" (Jeremiah 18:7, 8).

While God will never change his mission, his goal, or his plan for the redemption of humanity, he will and can change some particulars and methods in response to the prayers of his children. . . . For us to say that God will not or cannot do that is for us to freeze God's flexibility and to paralyze his power.
—Knofel Staton, *A Call to Prayer*

Central Theme: Even though the character of God is unchanging, prayer can change God's decisions and change circumstances.

Lesson Aim: Group members will examine biblical statements about the power of prayer in changing God's mind and will consider world, national, and personal circumstances that they choose to petition God to change.

Bible Background: 1 Samuel 15:29; 2 Kings 20:1–7, Jeremiah 18:7, 8; Ephesians 3:20, 21

For Further Study: Read Chapter One, "The Power of Prayer," in *A Call to Prayer.*

PLAN ONE

Classes

Materials You'll Need For This Session

Resource Sheets 1A and 1B, pens or pencils, Transparency 1A, chalkboard and chalk

BUILDING COMMUNITY

Distribute copies of Resource Sheet 1A and ask a class member to read the story. Then ask volunteers to tell how they think the Christians felt at points A, B, and C of the story. After posing the last question, ask, **What was the real (or hidden) prayer of the Christians?** The real prayer of the Christians was for God to show his power to the leader of the village.

Read and React
5–7 Minutes

Continue the discussion with some or all of these questions that probe more deeply into the puzzles of prayer, and prepare class members for today's session:
- What do you think of the request of the leader of the village?
- What does this tell us about how to pray when we want to persuade God to do something?
- What does this tell us about the sovereignty of God?
- What does this tell us about prayers that appear to be unanswered?

Consider interjecting any of these ideas if they don't surface. The leader of the village was testing God, which we are commanded not to do (Deuteronomy 6:16). This story shows how God in his wisdom and sovereignty often answers our prayers infinitely better than anything we could have dreamed of when we asked. We can ask God to change things, but we need to be open to his superior answers.

OPTION
Can of Worms Discussion
5–7 Minutes

Find a class member who has had a recent answer to prayer in which it seems that God's mind was changed or influenced by the prayer. Or you may wish to discuss an answered prayer that has occurred in your church family. **After the testimony, use questions such as those above to draw out members' thoughts.**

OPTION
Testimony
10 Minutes

CONSIDERING SCRIPTURE

Have class members choose partners and turn to *2 Kings 20:1–7.* One partner will assume the part of Hezekiah, and the other will play the part of Ace Interviewer for the television show *10½ Minutes.* The partners should read the

TV Interview
10 Minutes

Scripture together, and then the interviewer grills Hezekiah. Explain that Hezekiah was one of the last kings of Judah, one of the few good ones.

If you wish to provide questions for the interviewer, write the following on the chalkboard.

- So, what kind of a man doesn't die when God tells him to?
- What did you do to change God's mind?
- Does God like it when people brag about all they've done for him (v. 3) and cry a lot?
- Why do you think God told the good news that you would live another fifteen years to this guru Isaiah instead of you?
- Why, exactly, do you think God gave you an extra fifteen years of life?

After the interviews, focus on the last question. No reason is given. It seems that God did so because Hezekiah asked (v. 5). God mentioned other reasons, however, for delaying the capture of Judah—to uphold his reputation and that of King David (v. 6). This is the same reason Hezekiah used earlier in 2 Kings 19:19 in appealing to God to save Judah.

OPTION
Interview Skit
5 Minutes

During the interviews, circulate through the room and pick out one or two interviews that are going particularly well. Ask those class members to repeat their interview for the entire class.

Comparing Scripture
5 Minutes

Display <u>Transparency 1A</u> and **ask class members to reconcile the three Scriptures printed on the page.** (Comment that the best way to clarify the meaning of Scripture is to find another verse that seems to contradict it.) If you wish, resolve the discussion by reading the last paragraph of the introduction on page 7. **Explain that it isn't God's mind that is changed, but his choice of how to implement his will.**

TAKING THE NEXT STEP

If your class is less than eight people, work through the following activities together as a class. If you have more than eight, divide the class into small groups.

Prayer Writing
10 Minutes

Distribute copies of <u>Resource Sheet 1B.</u> Read Situation 1 and ask class members to **suggest how a person would pray according to the attitude described in A, and then according to attitude B and C.** Move on to Situation 2 and so on for as much time as you have.

Ask class members to write at the bottom of Resource Sheet 1B a news-oriented request or a personal request about which they feel burdened. After giving them a few minutes to write and think, ask them to write three prayers under it that follow the pattern of A, B, and C.

After class members are finished, lead them in prayer, asking God to show us how to interact with him better in our prayer life throughout this class. Ask for guidance for each class member about the topic they wrote on their sheet.

Groups

BUILDING COMMUNITY

1. Offer the following statement and ask group members to decide if they agree or disagree: **Our prayers can change God's mind.** After giving them a few minutes to think, ask those who agree to raise their hands. Ask a few to tell why, but do not respond. Then ask those who disagree to raise their hands. Ask a few to tell why, but do not respond. Bring up opposite points of view for each side. For example, turn to those who agreed, and say something like, **Does that mean that God's first choice was wrong?** Turn to those who disagree and ask, **Isn't God allowed to do as he pleases, changing his mind if he wants?** Your purpose at this point is not to come to a conclusion, but to raise questions.

2. OPTION: If the discussion is going well and you want to continue it, pose this new statement with which they may agree or disagree: **Prayer doesn't change God's mind, it changes our character.**

3. OPTION: Ask this question: **When in your life have you wished most that God would have changed his mind?**

CONSIDERING SCRIPTURE

Have a volunteer read *2 Kings 20:1–7,* and then pose these questions.

1. How would you have felt if you had been the prophet Isaiah, whose job it was to tell Hezekiah he was going to die? (Explain that Hezekiah was one of the last kings of Judah, one of the few good ones.)

2. Who is the man David, whose name is mentioned twice? (The legendary slayer of Goliath who became the greatest king of Israel, a man after God's own heart, Acts 13:22.)

3. What seemed to be the critical factors in changing God's mind to let Hezekiah live?

Materials You'll Need For This Session

Several newspapers, Resource Sheet 1A

OPTION
Accountability Partners
Have partners meet and agree to keep praying about at least one newspaper issue that touches their passions for God and for one personal circumstance they believe needs to be changed.

OPTION
Worship Ideas
• Read Psalm 8 together as an act of worship.

• Song suggestions: "Great and Mighty Is He," by Todd Pettygrove; "How Great Thou Art," by Carl Boberg; "Teach Me to Pray," by Albert S. Reitz

OPTION
Memory Verse
"Now to him who is able to do immeasurably more than all we ask or imagine, according to his power that is at work within us, to him be glory in the church and in Christ Jesus throughout all generations, for ever and ever! Amen" (Ephesians 3:20, 21).

Read *Jeremiah 18:7, 8; 1 Samuel 15:29; and Ephesians 3:20, 21;* or distribute copies of <u>Transparency 1A</u>.

4. How do you explain the seeming contradiction between the Jeremiah passage and the 1 Samuel passage?

5. Why is the majesty and sovereignty of God (Ephesians 3:20, 21) an important element in this debate?

6. Do you think less of God because he is willing to change his mind?

7. What would you say to people who think that if God changes his mind, it turns him into a "gimme machine" that Christians use to get what they want?

TAKING THE NEXT STEP

Distribute several newspapers (especially front pages).

1. Which of the issues mentioned here would you like to change God's mind about?

2. What personal concerns do you have that make you want to change God's mind?

3. OPTION. Distribute copies of <u>Resource Sheet 1A</u>. **What does this show us about how God answers prayers?**

Prayers

Knofel Staton relates this story:

Ron Morse witnessed an example of God's intervention years ago. He was working with some villagers in northern Thailand. That area was having the worst grasshopper plague they could remember. The leader of the village said to Ron, "You go away and gather your Christians and pray for three weeks that the grasshoppers will leave the Christians' fields but not the non-Christians' fields. If when you return in three weeks, the grasshoppers have left the Christians' fields and are still in the non-Christians' fields, I will help you lead this whole village to worship your Jesus." What a challenge! (A)

With earnestness and sincerity, the Christians prayed. Three weeks later Ron came into the village and was devastated by what he saw. It was obvious that the grasshoppers were still in the Christians' fields. In fact, there were more grasshoppers in those fields. (B)

But upon more careful examination, they found that the grasshoppers in the Christians' fields were only eating the weeds—they were not touching the rice—while the grasshoppers in the non-Christians' fields were eating the rice and not the weeds. There were so many grasshoppers in the Christians' fields that the dung they left fertilized the ground, so that there was an abundance of rice to feed the people. (C) We have an awesome God!

Describe how you think the Christians must have felt at point A in the story.

At point B:

At point C:

What do you think of the way God answered the real (or hidden) prayer of the Christians?

THE WAYS THAT COWBOYS PRAY

PRAYERS YOU WOULD PRAY IF . . .

A. you want your way and you'll badger God till the cows come home.

B. you ask God to change his mind, but you understand there's a thing or two he knows that you don't.

C. you figure God's gonna do what he's gonna do and nothing ain't gonna change it, sister.

If these situations came across the horizon, how would you pray about them in the three ways above?

SITUATION 1: If a government official, whom you know for a fact is corrupt, were elected?

SITUATION 2: If you were a candidate for a big promotion?

SITUATION 3: If your mother was having a biopsy tomorrow to find out if she has cancer?

The **POWER** Puzzle

GOD DOESN'T CHANGE HIS MIND?
"He who is the Glory of Israel does not lie or change his mind; for he is not a man, that he should change his mind" (1 Samuel 15:29).

GOD CAN CHANGE HIS MIND?
"If at any time I announce that a nation or kingdom is to be uprooted, torn down and destroyed, and if that nation I warned repents of its evil, then I will relent and not inflict on it the disaster I had planned" (Jeremiah 18:7, 8).

GOD IS SOVEREIGN
"Now to him who is able to do immeasurably more than all we ask or imagine, according to his power that is at work within us, to him be glory in the church and in Christ Jesus throughout all generations, for ever and ever! Amen" (Ephesians 3:20, 21).

Two

Down to Earth Prayer

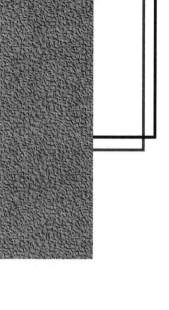

*M*ine is not an exemplary prayer life. Prayer meetings often depress me. Experienced participants utter their petitions with such eloquence and sincerity and at such length that I feel, well, outclassed. How dare I presume?

Jesus' brief prayer (Matthew 6:9–13) gives me license to try, inept as I am. According to Jesus, you don't have to be schooled in the subtleties of the truly religious to pray. You just have to want to talk with God, honestly, without ostentation.

Strutting your spirituality is the very thing that turns Jesus off. He nestles his comments on prayer between his guidelines for charity to the needy and for fasting. Concerning each of these three "acts of righteousness" the word is the same: don't strut your stuff (Matthew 6:1).

The prayer reminds us of who we are. We are the children of a powerful God, members of a powerful support group called the church.

—E. LeRoy Lawson, *A Call to Prayer*

Central Theme:	The model prayer encourages us to pray as a trusting yet humble child of God.
Lesson Aim:	Group members will examine the model prayer for its humble, down-to-earth tone and explore ways to be more real in their prayers.
Bible Background:	Matthew 6:9–13; Luke 15:11–32
For Further Study:	Read Chapter Two, "The Model Prayer" in *A Call to Prayer.*

Classes

Materials You'll Need For This Session

Resource Sheets 2A and 2B, pens or pencils, Transparency 2A

BUILDING COMMUNITY

Distribute copies of <u>Resource Sheet 2A</u> and read the instructions together. As class members begin to make their choices, help the class by telling on yourself. You might say something such as, "I used to act just like Genuine George. I look back now, and I can't believe it." **After giving them a few minutes, ask if any would like to tell the class which ones they've fallen prey to.** (Avoid finger pointing at other church members who may resemble these characters.)

Self-Evaluation
5 Minutes

Instead of distributing copies of Resource Sheet 2A to the entire class, gather a few energetic class members before class and show them the sheets. Have one person be a moderator for a Prayer Fashion Show, perhaps saying, **We have some fabulous people with us today. We all admire the way they pray. (Actually some of us think they're a bit stuffy—but then perhaps you'll recognize yourself in one of them.) First, we have. . . .** Then, have the class member playing Patty Prayer Warrior come forward and talk about her way of praying. (She can model a little on the stage, too, if she likes.) Do the same with the other three. **After they're finished, ask class members to figure out which character they most resemble now or have in the past.**

OPTION
Skit
10 Minutes

You may wish to **read the introduction to the group at this point.** It may encourage them to hear that Dr. LeRoy Lawson, a long-time minister and Christian-college president, struggles in this area.

OPTION
Guest Testimony
3 Minutes

CONSIDERING SCRIPTURE

 Display <u>Transparency 2A</u> and explain:
• The first column includes phrases from the Model Prayer (or Lord's Prayer).
• The middle column lists the down-to-earth tendency that phrase implies (according to LeRoy Lawson in *A Call to Prayer).*
• The right column lists an opposite, overly religious quality to which we could fall prey.
Ask class members to consider the column in the middle.

Chart Response
10–15 Minutes

Start with "personal" and ask them to suggest thoughts or phrases we could use in our prayers that would make them more personal. Do the same with each.

Here are some examples for each:

Personal—I thank you that you love me and watch out for me all day long.

Respectful—I'm making this request, but I understand that you have greater wisdom and can answer this better than I imagined.

Readiness to do God's will—I want whatever you want, God.

Trusting God—I don't understand your plan, but help me trust you anyway.

Simplicity—Keep me from chasing after a better car, a better house, a better job; but keep me focused on you and what you want to do with my life.

Willing to forgive—Help me to be more willing to forgive the people I can't seem to forgive. Help me to understand how much you've forgiven me.

Dependence—Forgive me when I don't call on you when I get into temptation that's too much for me. Help me to call on you for help immediately.

Praise—I honor you and glorify you. Help me to gain a sense of your majesty and power.

If any of the qualities stump them, ask them to suggest a phrase for the overly spiritual quality first. That may help. For example, the opposite of readiness to do God's will would be that familiar phrase: "I want what I want when I want it!"

OPTION
Chart Completion
10–15 Minutes

Display Transparency 2A. Cover the third column completely and cover the items in the middle column, but let the heading show. **Ask class members to suggest what down-to-earth quality the key phrase suggests.** As they make suggestions, uncover that quality and add their suggestions in the space under the ones provided. Do the same with the third column.

**Scripture Reading
& Meditation**
10 Minutes

Distribute Resource Sheet 2B. Introduce it by saying, **Scripture says the prodigal son "came to himself," and part of that seems to be his adopting the down-to-earth qualities in relation to his father. Let's look at some of these qualities and how the son learned them.** Ask one volunteer to read *Luke 15:11–32* and another to read Resource 2B.

Ask class members, who now have this story fresh in their minds, to sit quietly for a minute and put themselves in the place of the prodigal son. After a minute or two of silence, pray aloud, saying something like this: **Show us, God, how to relate to you in a personal way, but also with great respect. Help us to be ready to do your will instead of our own. Help us to trust you enough to** long only for simple things. Help us to be vulnerable enough to forgive others, depending on you for the protection we need. We give you honor and praise for your great love for us.

TAKING THE NEXT STEP

Once again, display <u>Transparency 2A</u>. Ask class members to choose a down-to-earth quality that they would like to incorporate in the way they pray. **Ask class members who are willing to tell the class what that quality is.**

Call out the name of each down-to-earth quality, and ask those who picked that quality to raise their hands. As the teacher, note which one they pick as it might be helpful in later sessions in this class.

Self-Evaluation
5 Minutes

OPTION
Survey
3–5 Minutes

*G*roups

BUILDING COMMUNITY

Read this example. **Brenda teaches second graders in Sunday school and she likes praying with them. But whenever the superintendent steps in for a minute and its time to pray, Brenda notices that she tries so hard to sound like an adult that she sounds like someone she and the kids don't even know.**

Ask these questions:
1. **In what circumstances is it most difficult for you to sound like yourself when you pray out loud?**

2. **When you pray silently, do you sound like yourself or do you try to pray like other people you've heard?**

3. **In what instances do you sound most like yourself when you pray?**

4. **Why is it important to sound like yourself when you pray?**

CONSIDERING SCRIPTURE

Read *Matthew 6:5–15.*

Show <u>Transparency 2A</u> to the group (or have one photocopy for each person) and explain that these down-to-earth qualities are exemplified in Jesus' Model Prayer. Read the chart if you wish.

Read *Luke 15:11–32* as a group.

1. **What evidence do we have that the prodigal son developed a more *personal* relationship with his father?**

2. **What evidence do we have that the prodigal son became more *respectful* of his father?**

3. **What evidence do we have that the prodigal son was *ready to do whatever his father wanted?***

> **Materials You'll Need For This Session**
>
> Transparency 2A

OPTION
Accountability Partners
Have accountability partners meet during the week to recall the ways we can relate to God in a more down-to-earth way. Encourage them to report any progress in any of these areas. Also ask them to tell how their reminders are working (Question 3 from "Taking the Next Step").

OPTION
Worship Ideas
• Read Psalm 131 together as an act of worship.

• Song Suggestions: "Humble Thyself in the Sight of the Lord," by Bob Hudson; "Thou Art Worthy," by Pauline Michael Mills; "Tis So Sweet to Trust in Jesus," by Louisa M.R. Stead and William J. Kirkpatrick

OPTION
Memory Verse
Group members who have never learned the Model Prayer may wish to do so. Those who have may need to review it.

---

4. What evidence do we have that the prodigal son *trusted* his father?

5. What evidence do we have that the prodigal son learned something about *simplicity* in life?

6. What evidence do we have that the prodigal son knew something about *forgiveness*?

7. What evidence do we have that the prodigal son learned *dependence* on his father?

8. What evidence do we have that the prodigal son honored his father *(praise)*?

TAKING THE NEXT STEP

1. Are you better at trusting God or at showing humble respect to God?

2. How do these two qualities seem to contradict each other?

3. What can we do to arm ourselves, when we pray, with the trusting yet humble attitude of the prodigal son?

Offer this idea to get them thinking: **Pause and wait in silence before we pray aloud or silently, gather our senses, and remember who we are—prodigal children.** Others, who can find a private place to pray, may want to lay prostrate on the floor in humility.

Prayer Actors & Actresses

Pick the cartoon character below that you have most resembled at some time in your Christian life. No doubt you were sincere in your efforts, but perhaps there was also that slightest bit of ostentation that leaked into your prayers.

‹ PATTY PRAYER WARRIOR

Tell her about a broken toenail and all at once she's holding your hand and praying for you.

EDGAR ELOQUENT ›

His Shakespearean prayers include words such as, "the blessings Thou hast bestowed upon us," "if the Lord doth tarry," "make haste to bless us," and "we have utterly gone astray."

‹ SUSAN SINCERITY

Her prayers are overly heartfelt as she says, "We just want to . . ." and "we just need to . . . ."

GENUINE GEORGE ›

His prayers are short, sweet, and simple with all the freshness of a new Christian, except that he's been a Christian for several years now and he's still praying the same prayers over and over.

What the Boy Learned

What the prodigal son learned parallels with what we can learn about praying more effectively.

ABOUT RESPECT

[The prodigal son] had tried writing his father out of his life's script. He could do it better his way. He had taken his inheritance and squandered it on the good life. He had immersed himself in the best the world offers. He had drunk its wine and sung its songs and had its women. When he sobered up in the pig sty, he was forced to admit there was only one abode where he really belonged. It was a sanctified place, special to him because his father dwelt there. His father was unlike anyone else he had encountered in his truancy, and his father's example and instruction towered above all other philosophies and so-called "truths" he had heard in his wanderings. There was about his father an aura, a difference— a holiness. He now revered his father's name as never before.

ABOUT WILLINGNESS AND FORGIVENESS

After he discerned his father's uniqueness, he was ready to do whatever his father asked him. Not daring to ask for his former place at the family table, he was willing to be a servant, if only he could live on his father's holdings. He was finished with demanding his rights, doing things his way, playing his own god. . . . Earlier the son had wanted only the father's money. Now he wanted to do his will. . . . American religiosity converts God into "a great cosmic public utility." He is useful for getting what we want. This divine public servant helps us to get our kingdom to come and our will to be done.

—From Chapter Two of *A Call to Prayer*

Praying Without Pretending

KEY PHRASE FROM THE MODEL PRAYER	DOWN-TO-EARTH QUALITY	OVERLY SPIRITUAL QUALITY
Father	personal	distant
in heaven, hallowed be your name	respectful	buddy-buddy
your kingdom come	readiness to do God's will	willing to do only what I want
your will be done	trusting God	protecting self
give us today our daily bread	simplicity	demanding a well-stocked pantry, house, church, career
forgive us our debts	willing to forgive	using God to get revenge
lead us not into temptation	dependence	toughing it out alone
for yours is the kingdom, the power, the glory forever	praise	focused only on my own needs

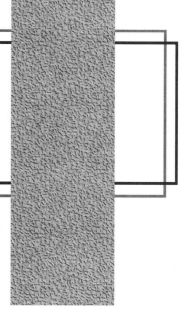

Three

Hindrances to Prayer

*P*rayer is probably the greatest privilege, opportunity, blessing, and responsibility that human beings enjoy. It enables us to communicate personally with the great God of this universe and makes available to us his unlimited power. . . .

If prayer is so readily available, so wondrously powerful, and so equally accessible, why is it . . . distinguished in its neglect by a large proportion of the church of Jesus Christ? Why do most believers find time to do nearly everything in the world except pray?

. . . Satan. Prayer is Satan's major enemy, and Satan is prayer's greatest foe. . . . In C.S. Lewis's *Screwtape Letters,* the demonic Screwtape admonished his nephew Wormwood to persevere in his efforts to lead people to Hell. Counteracting prayer is the primary strategy that he recommends. "Interfere at any price in any fashion when people start to pray, for real prayer is lethal to our cause."

— David Eubanks, *A Call to Prayer*

Central Theme: Prayer, our great resource in knowing God, is hindered by our neglect of God's Word, lack of commitment, spiritual laziness, selfish prayers, unrepented sin, and lack of faith.

Lesson Aim: Group members will examine various hindrances to their prayer life and pray for help in setting them aside.

Bible Background: Luke 5:16; Hebrews 5:7; James 4:3; Isaiah 59:2; Luke 17:5

For Further Study: Read Chapter Three, "Hindrances to Prayer," in *A Call to Prayer.*

Classes

Materials You'll Need For This Session

Resource Sheets 3A and 3B, paper, pens or pencils, Transparency 3A

BUILDING COMMUNITY

Divide the class into groups of three or four. Write the following on the chalkboard:

There once was a lady from _____,
Who found prayer to be _____.
She _____
And _____
And so it _____.

Explain that **as a group they should work together for three minutes to write a limerick based on a woman who has a lot of hindrances in her prayer life.** They can add many words to each line or just a few. Class members can work alone or with one partner if they prefer.

After three minutes, thank the groups for their efforts and ask a representative from each group to read their limerick.

Divide the class into groups of three or four, and **ask them to come up with five outrageous excuses for not praying.** The excuses should be of the "my dog ate my homework" type or perhaps terribly ironic, such as, "My new issue of *Prayer Digest* arrived, and I had to read it." After a minute or two, ask someone from each group to read the excuses.

CONSIDERING SCRIPTURE

Distribute Resource Sheet 3A. **Ask class members to underline the Scriptures there, putting a star by any that are especially meaningful and a question mark by any that are a little surprising.** Ask various class members to tell which verses they marked. Explain that people are often surprised that:

- so many prayers are recorded in the Bible—we think we have to make them all up.
- Jesus slipped off so often to be alone and pray (Luke 5:16)—we figure since he was God's Son, why did they have to talk?
- Jesus cried out in prayer and seemed to struggle in it (Hebrews

Limerick Writing
5–7 Minutes

OPTION
Making Up Excuses
5–7 Minutes

Coding Scripture
10 Minutes

5:7)—we figure since Jesus was divine, what struggles could he have had?

- we shouldn't focus on our own desires in prayer (James 4:3)—isn't that what prayer is for, to get us out of jams?
- our unrepented sins can separate us from God (Isaiah 59:2)—we figure Jesus died on the cross for our sins, so what's the problem?
- one way to increase our faith is to ask God to increase it (Luke 17:5)—we figure it should be more difficult than that.

OPTION
Analyzing Hindrances
3–5 Minutes

Ask class members if they think the hindrances listed on Resource Sheet 3A should come in a particular order. Do some result from the others? Lack of commitment, spiritual laziness, and lack of faith were listed last because they seem to be results of the others. Do they agree?

OPTION
Contrasting Concepts
10–15 Minutes

Display Transparency 3A. **Ask class members to help you list a corresponding help (probably the opposite of the hindrance) in the middle column beside each hindrance.** Then ask them to make suggestions for specific ways to carry out that help for prayer, listing their responses in the right column. For example:

HINDRANCES	HELPS	IDEAS
NEGLECT OF GOD'S WORD	Study God's Word	• Use a read-the-Bible-in-a-year program. • Read one section of a gospel every Saturday.

OPTION
More Thorough Scripture Study
10–20 Minutes

If you would like to include more direct study of the Scripture, display Transparency 3A and **ask class members to look up the expanded list of Scriptures listed in the left column.** If you don't wish to use the other two columns, place a sheet of paper over them so they aren't distracting. Or, look up Scriptures for topics that class members find to be more of a struggle.

Playing Screwtape's Role
15 Minutes

Direct the class members' attention to Resource Sheet 3A again and explain that these are general categories only. **Satan has specific, crafty ways of distracting us and alienating us from prayer.** Read the last paragraph of the introduction on page 31 and **explain that class members will assume the role of Screwtape and come up with specific ways of implementing these six hindrances against the average Christian.**

If the class is larger than eight, divide the class into two or more groups, assigning one group the first three hindrances and the other group the second three. After the groups are finished, ask them to report back.

Taking the Next Step

🔲 **Divide the class into groups of four and ask them to take turns telling the group how the information in today's session has affected them.** Write these two questions on the chalkboard for them to answer:
- What is hindering my prayer life?
- What is God leading me to do about it?

🔲 Distribute paper and ask class members to write a prayer to God, naming the hindrances they feel most keenly and asking for his help.

🔲 Distribute Resource Sheet 3B. **Ask the class to read it together as a closing prayer.** Explain that after they read, "Amen," the class will remain in silence for a minute or two. Then you will say something like, "Dismissed" or "Thank you for your attention."

Prayer Groups
10–15 Minutes

Option
Prayer Writing
3–5 Minutes

Group Closing Prayer
5 Minutes

PLAN TWO

BUILDING COMMUNITY

1. Distribute index cards or small pieces of paper and ask group members to write the answer to this question on the card: **What is the most difficult thing for you about prayer?** After they've written their answer, ask them to tuck this card away in a pocket or purse.

2. OPTION: Distribute copies of <u>Resource Sheet 3B</u> and read it aloud. Ask group members to underline a sentence or two that best describes their difficulties with prayer. Have them talk with a partner about what they underlined.

CONSIDERING SCRIPTURE

Distribute copies of <u>Resource Sheet 3A</u> and read it aloud.

1. How are prayer and Bible study good complements to each other?

2. What kinds of prayer do we pray other than prayers for ourselves?

3. What do you do if you've sinned and you want to repent, but you know you haven't truly repented in your heart?

4. Why is it imperative that busy people pray?

5. Do you have a place where you can go to God and "offer up prayers and petitions with loud cries and tears"?

6. How do you think you would behave differently if your faith were increased? (Encourage group members to consider temptations and unfulfilled dreams.)

7. Why do you think "lack of time" isn't listed as a hindrance?

Materials You'll Need For This Session

Index cards or small pieces of paper

OPTION
Accountability Partners
Have partners meet and pray about their hindrances, especially unrepented sin. Encourage them to share their temptations and suggest ways of helping each other fight them.

OPTION
Worship Ideas
• Read Psalm 145 together as an act of worship.

• Song Suggestions: "Seek Ye First the Kingdom of God," by Karen Lafferty; "Have Thine Own Way, Lord," by Adelaide A. Pollard; "Bless His Holy Name" by Andrae Crouch

OPTION
Memory Verse
"During the days of Jesus' life on earth, he offered up prayers and petitions with loud cries and tears" (Hebrews 5:7).

8. Are there other hindrances you can think of that aren't listed? (Ask group members to look at the index cards they filled out at the beginning of the session and compare what's written there with the hindrances listed. If group members mention hindrances and difficulties not included in the list on Resource 3A, ask others to offer helpful feedback for that hindrance.)

TAKING THE NEXT STEP

1. What hindrance do you believe you're most ready to tackle?

2. How do you think God will help you address it?

Hindrances to Prayer

NEGLECT OF GOD'S WORD

If we stay away from God's Word, we miss some of the most beautiful, powerful, and persuasive prayers ever prayed: Moses' prayers in behalf of Israel, David's prayers in the Psalms, Jesus' prayers, especially the ones in John 17 and in the garden of Gethsemane. Apart from the Bible, how can we develop the concepts and language of prayer?

PRAYING SELFISHLY

"When you ask, you do not receive, because you ask with wrong motives, that you may spend what you get on your pleasures" (James 4:3). Prayer is not looking upon God as the great Santa Claus in the sky who will give us everything on our wish list. The goal of our lives and our prayers should be to glorify the Lord and to see his authority and kingdom spread over all the earth.

UNREPENTED SIN

God has made clear that he will not respond to the unrepentant sinner. Isaiah prophesied to the sinful Israelites, "But your iniquities have separated you from your God; your sins have hidden his face from you, so that he will not hear" (Isaiah 59:2). It is not the fact that we have sinned that obstructs our prayers. Unrepented, unconfessed sin is the problem, especially an unforgiving spirit. Nothing is more self-destructive than a critical, condemning, and implacable attitude. How can we communicate with a merciful and forgiving God if we hold malice, ill will, and resentment in our hearts toward others?

LACK OF COMMITMENT

The busier our Lord was, the more he prayed. Although he had no sin to confess, he "often withdrew to lonely places and prayed" (Luke 5:16). Crowds pressed him so intensely that he did not always have time to eat, but he always found time to pray. He prayed all night on many occasions.

SPIRITUAL LAZINESS

We live in the age of the "quick fix" and instant gratification. Too many Christians want maximum spiritual results without expending more than minimal spiritual energy. A powerful prayer life often develops out of struggle. "During the days of Jesus' life on earth, he offered up prayers and petitions with loud cries and tears" (Hebrews 5:7). No one will learn from Jesus that prayer is an easy road.

LACK OF FAITH

Ironic as it may seem, we can pray for increased faith to pray more effectively. The apostles said to the Lord, "Increase our faith!" (Luke 17:5).

—Adapted from Chapter Three of *A Call to Prayer*

The Difficulties of Praying

Why, O Lord, is it so hard for me to keep my heart directed toward you? Why do the many little things I want to do, and the many people I know, keep crowding into my mind, even during the hours that I am totally free to be with you and you alone? Why does my mind wander off in so many directions, and why does my heart desire the things that lead me astray? Are you not enough for me? Do I keep doubting your love and care, your mercy and grace? Do I keep wondering, in the centre of my being, whether you will give me all I need if I just keep my eyes on you?

Please accept my distractions, my fatigue, my irritations, and my faithless wanderings. You know me more deeply and fully than I know myself. You love me with a greater love than I can love myself. You even offer me more than I can desire. Look at me, see me in all my misery and inner confusion, and let me sense your presence in the midst of my turmoil. All I can do is show myself to you. Yet, I am afraid to do so. I am afraid that you will reject me. But I know—with the knowledge of faith—that you desire to give me your love. The only thing you ask of me is not to hide from you, not to run away in despair, not to act as if you were a relentless despot.

Take my tired body, my confused mind, and my restless soul into your arms and give me rest, simple quiet rest. Do I ask too much too soon? I should not worry about that. You will let me know. Come, Lord Jesus, come. Amen.

—Henri Nouwen
A Cry For Mercy

Exploring Hindrances

HINDRANCES	HELPS	IDEAS
NEGLECT OF GOD'S WORD An Example of one of . . . Daniel's prayers: Daniel 9:4–19 Jesus' prayers: John 17 Paul's prayers: Philippians 1:9–11 **PRAYING SELFISHLY** John 14:13 2 Thessalonians 3:1, 2, 5 James 4:3 **UNREPENTED SIN** Isaiah 59:2 Mark 11:25 James 5:16 1 John 1:9 **LACK OF COMMITMENT** Luke 5:16 James 4:2 **SPIRITUAL LAZINESS** Nehemiah 1:4; 2:4 Hebrews 5:7 Luke 22:44 Ephesians 6:18 **LACK OF FAITH** Luke 17:5 Matthew 21:21, 22 Mark 9:23, 24 Luke 11:11–13		

Four

Putting Muscle Into Prayer

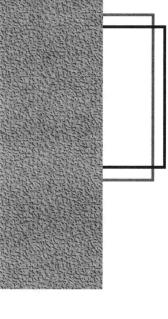

*T*he basic difference between Christians of the first century and those of this century is that they prayed while we talk about prayer. They prayed and the building shook, the Holy Spirit possessed them, and they spoke the name of Jesus in boldness! We talk about prayer, but a host of barriers arise and we just don't get to it.

Jesus prayed at his baptism and the Holy Spirit came upon him. He spent the night in prayer before selecting the twelve men in whom he would invest his life. He called his men to pray. They responded by pleading, "Lord, teach us to pray." He prayed and was transfigured. He prayed and Lazarus emerged from the grave, alive! He prayed in the garden when all had deserted him. From the cross, Jesus prayed for his enemies.

When people most sought Christ, he most sought God. "In the early morning, while it was still dark, He arose and went out and departed to a lonely place, and was praying there. . . . And they found Him and said to Him, 'Everyone is looking for You'" (Mark 1:35, 37, *New American Standard Bible*).

—Adapted from Robert Yawberg, *A Call to Prayer*

Central Theme: Christians can weave prayer in and out of their daily routine so that there's no inappropriate time for prayer.

Lesson Aim: Group members will look at the pattern of prayer in Jesus' life and examine how prayer can fit in the patterns of their lives.

Bible Background: 1 Thessalonians 5:17; Luke 3:21, 22; 6:12–16; 9:18; 9:28–36; 11:1; 22:39–46; 23:34; John 11:38–44

For Further Study: Read Chapter Four, "Pray for Revival," and Chapter Seven, "My House Will Be Called a House of Prayer," in *A Call to Prayer.*

Classes

Materials You'll Need For This Session

Resource Sheets 4A–4C, pens or pencils, Transparency 4A

BUILDING COMMUNITY

Read this story to the class.

Everyone at the attorney's office was rushing toward a 5:00 P.M. court deadline. Kim, the secretary, said under her breath, "God, give me strength and ability to do this accurately and quickly."

"What did you say?" asked her co-worker.

Kim laughed and said, "I was just praying."

Her co-worker looked at her in ridicule. "This is a stupid time to pray. You should be working."

Explain, **In truth, there are never inappropriate times to pray, but we think there are.** Ask, **What are those situations, and why do we think they're inappropriate?** (Most of the situations occur only if we substitute prayer for what we ought to be doing: working hard, asking forgiveness, helping someone out. Actually, we can do any of these things and pray at the same time.)

Ask, **What is the oddest situation in which you've ever prayed?**

Try to draw out stories that move beyond asking for help in dire need or expressing spontaneous thanks or praise at a beautiful sunset. Note prayer during the everyday moments of life.

CONSIDERING SCRIPTURE

Display <u>Transparency 4A</u> and work through the first row of the chart with the entire class. **First, have a class member look up the Scripture passage in the left column and read it.** This passage tells about Jesus' baptism, which is noted on the chart. Ask, **What was Jesus doing when the heavens opened?** Luke is the only gospel writer that notes that Jesus was praying when the heavens opened and God spoke. **In the next column, a general classification is listed for this event:** Jesus was at a spiritual-marker event in his life. **Then read the common spiritual markers listed in the third column and ask class members to list others they can think of.** Explain that they will find similar types of answers to fill in the rest of the chart.

Divide the class into groups of four and assign each group one or more of the Scripture passages listed on the left. Give

Respond to the Story
5–7 Minutes

OPTION
Testimony Question
5 Minutes

Small Group Discussion
15 Minutes

them about five minutes to work, and then ask each group to report back. As they do so, write their findings on the transparency. They might note that Jesus prayed:

- before making decisions, such as choosing the twelve apostles
- after successful situations, such as the feeding of the 5000
- as God used him to reveal divine power and glory (the transfiguration)
- when asked to teach people to pray
- before calling on God's power (raising Lazarus)
- when faced with an incredible challenge (in the garden before the cross)
- when treated unfairly by his enemies (on the cross).

Ask a volunteer to read the Scripture and the question at the bottom of the transparency. Ask class members for their thoughts.

Note that Jesus prayed in all sorts of daily events. He illustrated well the theme verse for today, 1 Thessalonians 5:17, "Pray continually."

OPTION
Class Works Together
15–20 Minutes

If your class is small or if you've done small group work frequently, ask volunteers to be ready to read the passages at the appropriate time. Work through the chart together as a class.

Brainstorming
5 Minutes

Distribute copies of Resource Sheet 4A and have a volunteer read it. **Ask class members to help you brainstorm a list of events, based on Robert Yawberg's experiences, in which prayer is helpful.**

TAKING THE NEXT STEP

Cartoon Strip
10–15 Minutes

Refer to the last paragraph of Resource Sheet 4A, and explain that many people would consider it odd to pray while cooking, with all the noise and clatter of a kitchen. Yet Brother Lawrence did that as part of his practice of the presence of God.

Distribute pencils and copies of Resource Sheet 4B and ask class members to draw a cartoon of themselves praying at a moment they never thought of praying before. They may either:

- draw a strip so they can set up the situation that leads to this odd moment for prayer, or
- fill in one or two frames with a picture that shows them praying in a situation in which people don't normally pray.

Encourage them to use stick figures only. If they try to be too artistic, it will take too long and they will create a standard that is difficult for all class members to follow. **After allowing them a few minutes to draw, ask volunteers to show their cartoons to each other.** If they seem reluctant, have them show the cartoons only to the person sitting next to them.

If your class would be especially intimidated by drawing the cartoons, have them **work in groups of two to four to produce the cartoons.** Stress that anything more than stick figures is not necessary. Have them report back to the entire class.

OPTION
Group Cartoons
10–15 Minutes

Distribute Resource Sheet 4C and read it to the class. **Ask class members to underline the creative ways that the author wove prayer into the daily events of life.**

OPTION
Read and React
5–10 Minutes

After using Transparency 4A as stated above, ask these questions: **What difference does it make when you pray after a success? Before making choices? Before serving others? While facing enemies?** Say, **Sometimes we feel it makes little difference. Why is that?**
Explain that, **Prayer is a relationship skill. It takes us awhile to get comfortable with it. We don't pray to get answers as you would put a coin into a candy machine to get candy. We pray to develop a relationship with God. We may need to wait and listen, just as we do with our friends.**

OPTION
Discussion Questions
5–7 Minutes

Ask class members to pick an event or odd moment in their lives in which they would like to start praying. Have them choose a partner in the class and pray with that person about remembering to pray the next time they're in that situation.

Prayer Time
3 Minutes

Groups

BUILDING COMMUNITY

1. Why do you think Christians are more likely to talk about prayer than to pray?

2. What fears are involved?

3. OPTION: What would it take to transfer the good feeling we sometimes have when we talk about prayer to a time of actually praying?

CONSIDERING SCRIPTURE

Assign a Scripture verse to each person, and ask everyone to have it ready at the appropriate time: *Luke 3:21, 22; 6:12–16; 9:18; 9:28–36; 11:1; 22:39–46; 23:34; John 11:38–44; and 1 Thessalonians 5:17.*

1. Read *Luke 3:21, 22.*
What was Jesus doing during his baptism when the heavens opened and God spoke?

2. Read *Luke 6:12–16.*
What do you imagine were specific things about which Jesus prayed the night before he chose the twelve apostles?

3. Read *Luke 9:18* and remind them that this occurred just after Jesus fed the 5,000 and had become enormously popular.
Why, in the midst of success, is it so difficult for us to pray?

4. **What can we pray about in the midst of success?**

5. Read *Luke 9:28–36.*
What was Jesus doing when his face changed during the transfiguration?

6. **In what ways does praying change us?**

Materials You'll Need For This Session

Resource Sheets 4A, 4C

Accountability Partners

Have partners meet and discuss with each other what odd moments they've been able to pray and practice God's presence. Those who have forgotten can refresh their minds and perhaps choose different moments to target for this.

OPTION

Worship Ideas

• Read Psalm 34 together as an act of worship.

• Song Suggestions: "Psalm 34:1" ("I Will Bless the Lord at All Times"); "Father, I Adore You," by Terrye Coelho; "Spirit of the Living God," by Dan Iverson

OPTION

Memory Verse

"Pray continually" or "Pray without ceasing" *(King James Version)* (1 Thessalonians 5:17).

7. Read *Luke 11:1*.
Do you believe it's actually more difficult to pray than to talk about how to pray? Why or why not?

8. Read *John 11:38–44*.
Wasn't Jesus powerful enough to raise Lazarus without praying aloud? What purposes would Jesus have had for praying out loud rather than silently?

9. Read *Luke 22:39–46*.
What do you suppose Jesus "got out of" this prayer session?

10. Read *Luke 23:34*.
How do you think Jesus was able to pray such a prayer while hanging on the cross?

11. Read *1 Thessalonians 5:17*.
How does one go about doing this?

12. OPTION. To illustrate the answer to Question 11, distribute copies of Resource Sheet 4C and note especially the fourth and fifth paragraphs.

TAKING THE NEXT STEP

Distribute Resource Sheet 4A and ask a volunteer to read the first three paragraphs. Or, read this to the group without distributing it.

1. **What can our group (or our accountability partners) learn from these experiences?**

2. Read the last paragraph of Resource Sheet 4A. **What would it take for you to be able to pray as Brother Lawrence did, with all the "noise and clatter of my kitchen"?**

3. **In what odd moments of your life could you enjoy God's presence, talking to him and listening in silence?**

EXPERIENCES IN Prayer

Our church broke ground for a long-awaited building program in 1973. Days later, we learned the promised bank loan was not available. We were driven to prayer. Having heard of the early morning prayer meetings in Korea, I announced on a Sunday morning, "We will meet at 5:30 A.M. for prayer tomorrow and continue daily until we find the Lord's answer to our dilemma."

Little did we know it would require over forty consecutive days of such prayer discipline before we gained direction. The answer came unexpectedly as eighty families from our congregation were led to establish a new work in the central city of Fort Wayne. My family went with the new work. The mother church later completed the long-awaited building. Without daily prayer over a sustained period of time, we would have missed God's open door.

Rather than assemble at the building each midweek, Marilyn and I decided to invite a few people to our home. We selected those recently baptized and others who had inquired about the church. For the past fifteen years, we have continued to meet with groups of ten or twelve for a period of six weeks. I teach them biblical truths on what it means to seriously follow Jesus. I pray with the men and Marilyn prays with the women as we close each session. There, with a few newfound friends, needs are confessed and prayers spoken. Praying together specifically for one another has had a profound effect on this congregation.

✦ ✦ ✦

Above all, prayer is practicing the presence of Jesus. It is not merely a set hour. It may not be on our knees or even with eyes closed. To pray without ceasing should be our goal. To awaken with, "Lord, good morning. I invite you to control my life today." And moment by moment to speak often and listen much as the Spirit of Jesus dwells in us. Brother Lawrence in *The Practice of the Presence of God* says it well. "The time of business does not differ with me from the time of prayer; and, in the noise and clatter of my kitchen I possess God in as great tranquillity as if I were on my knees at the blessed sacrament."

—Adapted from Robert Yawberg, *A Call to Prayer*

See You in the Funny Papers!

NO TIME TO *Pray?*

Structure. Time for others. Extensive Bible study. Regular quiet times. Long, in-depth conversations . . .

These days gone by are my "B.K." days—Before Kids! Now my days are drastically different as a mother with three small children. I spend my waking hours meeting the varying needs of three precious souls.

The adjustment from being employed outside my home to my present choice, "household watcher" (Proverbs 31:27), has required personal struggle. Praise God, I am grateful that I now have a clear, concrete understanding of the highest and most significant of ministries. That ministry is prayer. Prayer dispels the error that only "doing" can be significant. Prayer instead places significance on involvement in the ultimate battle between the spiritual forces of evil and God (Ephesians 6:12).

The wife and mother has the tremendous opportunity to commit herself to becoming a home prayer warrior. Although her role has physical restraints, it often leaves her heart free to do spiritual battle for the Great Commission. What a beautiful, powerful sight—busy, committed hands with a boundless heart! This mother heart, with its immeasurable attributes of perseverance and faith, is moldable material for the significant ministry of prayer.

Your desire as a prayer warrior is for prayer to become an involuntary reflex in response to the challenges of the day. Think through a typical day's sights and happenings. Perhaps as you awaken, having enjoyed the blessing of a good night's rest (Psalm 4:8), your heart can turn to those people you know who are experiencing the pain of the inability to sleep due to a stressful family situation. As you prepare the morning breakfast, your heart can be moved to intercede on behalf of the people of Russia, whose daily food is not a certainty (James 2:15). As your children prepare for school, you sense God's prompting to pray for their teachers, administrators, and school personnel as well as your friends and their children's school-day needs (Philippians 1:3).

What happens in your heart as you stand waiting in the grocery checkout line and your eye catches the headlines of newspaper or periodicals? Instead of succumbing to doubt, frustration, or fear, quickly turn your thoughts into prayer regarding what you have seen. What do you do with your thoughts when you walk down the street and are aware that the teenagers you see are engaging in activities of darkness? Begin to intercede for them. Every act of meeting a need or performing a chore can be seen as a prompting to pray.

When in doubt as to what is best to pray, effective prayers reflect Jesus' concern: "Thy kingdom come" (Matthew 6:10). We do not need to be consumed by concern over our inability to frame impressive, power-packed prayers—the issue is the response of our hearts.

—Adapted from Javonda Barnes, *A Call to Prayer*

Jesus, THE CONSTANT PRAY-ER

Situation in Jesus' life in which he prayed	Type of event	When do you experience this type of event?
Luke 3:21, 22 (Jesus' baptism)	• A spiritual marker in his life	• Decision to start a through-the-Bible-in-a-year study program • Decision to stop painful habit •
Luke 6:12–16		
Luke 9:18		
Luke 9:28–36		
Luke 11:1		
John 11:38–44		
Luke 22:39–46		
Luke 23:34		

When people most sought Christ, he most sought God. "In the early morning, while it was still dark, He arose and went out and departed to a lonely place, and was praying there. . . . And they found Him, and said to Him, 'Everyone is looking for You'" (Mark 1:35, 37, NASB).

• When we are "sought after," whom or what do we seek?

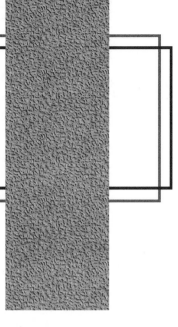

Five

Intimacy With God

*M*ost churches are busy churches. . . . We are often in danger of choosing the important over the essential. Christian service is important. Serving on committees and developing programs that help the church carry out its mission is vital. But we tend to be so activity-oriented we often forget that the heart of Christianity is a relationship with a person, Jesus Christ. . . .

In our prayer lives we often overlook this personal relationship with the Lord. We come to God with our lists. We pray for the sick, the missionaries, our country, the church, our families, our finances—and the list continues. And properly so. We ought to be praying for all of these individuals and situations on a daily basis. But too often that is where our prayers end. What happened to relationship? Where in our prayers have we drawn near to God?

Restoring this missing element in our prayer lives will rejuvenate us spiritually and enable us to carry on in our service to the Lord.

—David Butts, *A Call to Prayer*

Central Theme: Prayer is one of the primary tools for building an intimate relationship with God.

Lesson Aim: Group members will explore how the psalmist built intimacy with God through prayer and will consider ways they can build intimacy with God.

Bible Background: Psalm 63:1–8

For Further Study: Read Chapter Five, "Prayer as Intimacy With God," in *A Call to Prayer.*

Classes

BUILDING COMMUNITY

Distribute copies of <u>Resource Sheet 5A</u> and ask class members to fill out the quiz. After allowing a few minutes, ask those who consider themselves Martha-types to make a motion as if sweeping a floor at the count of three. Ask those who consider themselves Mary-types to make a motion as if praying, at the count of three. Ask them to notice how people they know respond. (Be prepared to explain to any who are unfamiliar with the story of Mary and Martha that Martha is considered a doer, while Mary was more interested in listening to Jesus, hence spiritual things. For their story, see Luke 10:38–42. Mary was also quite unconventional, because women weren't supposed to concern themselves with spiritual discussions in public.)

Count to three and let class members make their appropriate motions. Then ask if anyone disagrees with the motion their friend or spouse made. Ask, **Do you see your friends differently than they see themselves?** Allow a few to answer.

You can simply ask them to categorize themselves and not use Resource Sheet 5A.

Write this statement on the chalkboard: **It's difficult for busy people to be spiritual too.** Ask those who agree to raise their hands, and ask them why they chose that position. Ask those who disagree to raise their hands, and ask them why they chose that position. **After some discussion, explain that this session is not going to try to prove one side or another, just raise discussion about what is required to become intimate with God.**

CONSIDERING SCRIPTURE

Ask class members to turn to **_Psalm 63:1–8,_** and have a volunteer read it aloud. Then ask this question: **What clues does this passage give you to explain David's intimacy with God?** Encourage them to try to find one clue per verse. Here are some clues they may find.

• **_Expressing desire for intimacy (v. 1)._** David admitted that

---

Categorizing Self
5–7 Minutes

Materials You'll Need For This Session

Resource Sheets 5A and 5B, pens or pencils, paper, Transparency 5A, index cards, colored pens or pencils, chalkboard

OPTION

OPTION
Agree–Disagree
5–7 Minutes

Thematic Study
10–15 Minutes

he hungered for intimacy with God, implying that he didn't have it at that moment but was used to it enough that he missed it.

• *Remembering past times of intimacy (v. 2).* David referred back to times of worship in which he had sensed God's intimacy. He looked back with grateful anticipation of a similar experience, rather than with regret that he wasn't experiencing it again. As we pray and worship, we may experience joy, tears, exhilaration, or fear, but we may try to avoid an encounter with God.

• *Praising God (vv. 3, 4).* The more we know God, the more we desire to praise him and find reasons to praise him. Worship is not reserved only for corporate worship services; it also occurs in solitude with God.

• *Spontaneous times with God (v. 6).* Besides the times we set aside to be with God, we can practice his presence as we lie down on our bed and as we awake. What was a mere bedroom becomes a sanctuary.

• *Picturing our dependence on God (vv. 7, 8).* David expressed how dependent he was on God by picturing God as a huge bird with wings and himself as someone who could live under those wings. We too can picture how dependent we are on God.

OPTION
A Closer Look at Praise
5–10 Minutes

Praising God can be difficult for some people because they haven't seen it modeled well in prayer. **You may wish to display <u>Transparency 5A</u> and look up some of the passages together. Encourage class members to use these simple concepts as a basis for praising God.**

OPTION
Key Words
10 Minutes

Have class members turn to Psalm 63:1–8 and read it aloud. Ask them to pick out ten key words from this passage. After allowing a few minutes, ask for their suggestions and write them on the chalkboard. Ask, **What do these key words tell us about intimacy with God?** Tie in their responses with the points above.

OPTION
Paraphrase
10–15 Minutes

Distribute paper and pencils and have class members turn to Psalm 63:1–8. Read it together once aloud and then ask class members to paraphrase it—to reword it in such a way that it sounds like they had said it themselves.

OPTION
Half and Half
15–25 Minutes

If you wish, do both of the above activities. **Half of the class can study Psalm 63 and the other half can paraphrase it.** Then they can share with each other what they've found.

TAKING THE NEXT STEP

Distribute copies of Resource Sheet 5B and have a volunteer read it aloud. Distribute index cards, and put colored pens in a central place. **Ask class members to choose one of the two verses mentioned on the sheet and to make a prayer card with that verse on it.** They can carry this with them to remember to pray this verse. Encourage them to give the card a look that is appealing to them, using as many colored markers as they wish.

Distribute paper, pens, and colored pens, and **ask class members to design a symbol to stand for intimacy with God.** It can be very simple, a doodle that uses familiar symbols such as a heart or Christian symbols. After allowing them a few minutes to work, ask volunteers to show their work.

Close in prayer, paraphrasing Philippians 3:10, 11, in a manner such as this: **We want to know Christ and the power of his resurrection. We want to know something of what it means to share in his sufferings. We want to become like him in his death, dying to ourselves, and to look forward to attaining the resurrection from the dead.**

Prayer Cards
10 Minutes

OPTION
Symbol Design
7–10 Minutes

Prayer Time
3 Minutes

Groups

BUILDING COMMUNITY

1. Hold up colored pens or several pieces of construction paper, and ask group members to tell which color they associate most with intimacy with God. Give them a few minutes to think. After each person has expressed an opinion, ask group members to tell why they chose the color they did.

Listen for any thoughts that are similar to qualities that will come up later. Comment on the similarity then.

2. OPTION: **When is life like a dry and weary land?**

3. OPTION: Choose someone who you know has an intimate relationship with God (you don't have to reveal the name) and tell what evidence you see of that.

CONSIDERING SCRIPTURE

Read *Psalm 63:1–8.*

1. What does it mean to thirst for God?

2. Would it be easy for you to tell God that you are thirsty for him?

3. With what attitude does David seem to recall his mountaintop experience with God (v. 2)?

4. Why do we often speak with sadness about past mountaintop experiences?

5. How was David's praise much more than an intellectual assent to God's greatness? (David used his lips and hands. He worshiped God with his intellect, his body, his emotions.)

6. What kinds of thoughts might David have had of God in the night?

7. What pictures did David offer of his dependence on God?

> **Materials You'll Need For This Session**
>
> Colored pens or construction paper

OPTION
Accountability Partners

Have accountability partners meet during the week to share how they felt about the session on intimacy with God. Did it make them uncomfortable? If so, why? If they felt comfortable, ask them to share their progress with their group. Did they like their word picture? Why or why not?

OPTION
Worship Ideas

• Read Psalm 42 together as an act of worship.

• Song suggestions: "Thy Loving Kindness"; "Psalm 63," by Matthew Ward and Richard Souther; "Draw Me Nearer," by Fanny J. Crosby and William H. Doane

OPTION
Memory Verse

"O God, you are my God, earnestly I seek you; my soul thirsts for you, my body longs for you, in a dry and weary land where there is no water" (Psalm 63:1).

8. **How does expressing our dependence on God increase our intimacy with God?**

9. **Which verse in this passage do you like best? Why?**

TAKING THE NEXT STEP

Ask group members, **What word picture would you create to express intimacy with God?**

Remind group members that David's word pictures came out of his culture—large birds, livestock herders who hiked up and down rocks and hills. If your class members' world involves computers or stock invoices or saucepans, those can be used in word pictures.

Allow group members a few minutes and then ask some of them to share their word pictures. This is important because one person may find another's word picture even more helpful than her own.

Are you a

Mary clone OR A *Martha* clone?

1. At a church dinner, I would rather:
   ☐ serve dinner (a)
   ☐ say the blessing (b)

2. If I had volunteered to teach junior high kids in VBS, I would have volunteered to:
   ☐ work on crafts or recreation (a)
   ☐ teach the Bible study (a/b)
   ☐ pray for the brave person teaching (b)

3. Assuming I had children, if I were to have devotions with them, it would be:
   ☐ a casual conversation while hiking or tossing a baseball or _____ (a)
   ☐ reading the Bible together and talking about it (b)

4. Given a huge decision to make, I ask God to:
   ☐ give me a sign (a)
   ☐ give me a sense of his answer to my prayer (b)

If you checked mostly (a), consider yourself a Martha. (Admittedly, she's gotten a bad rap, so don't take it too hard.) If you check mostly (b), consider yourself a Mary.

Intimacy With God
STARTER KIT

How can we develop passion for God? Here are some practical ideas.

❤ *Spend Time With People in Love With God*

Wouldn't it have been great to spend time with David as he worshiped and prayed? In addition to learning from him, perhaps some of his passion for God would be contagious. I've had the privilege of praying with a number of men and women who have an intimate walk with the Lord. If I know that any of these brothers or sisters are going to be within driving distance, I try to get away to spend time with them in prayer. I always come away refreshed and encouraged in my own quest. You probably have someone in your church from whom you could learn as you pray together.

❤ *Spend More Time With God*

This class alone will not give you a greater intimacy with God. The only thing that will do that is to actually spend more time with him. The more we know him, the more we love him and the more we will want to be with him.

❤ *Get to Know Him More in His Word*

The Bible is not just intended to give us facts and doctrine. Its purpose is to reveal God. Jesus criticized the Pharisees because they studied the Bible, which spoke of Jesus, but would not come to him.

Use the Bible as a place of prayer. As the Word of God teaches you something about the nature of God, stop and praise God for what you just learned about him. Praying through the Bible can be one of the greatest experiences of your life. Here are some examples:

• *John 17:26*—At the close of his great high priestly prayer, Jesus prays to his Father on behalf of his disciples: "I have made you known to them, and will continue to make you known in order that the love you have for me may be in them and that I myself may be in them." Jesus prayed that the love the Father has for him would be in us.

• *Philippians 3:10, 11*—"I want to know Christ and the power of his resurrection and the fellowship of sharing in his sufferings, becoming like him in his death, and so, somehow, to attain to the resurrection from the dead." Can you imagine this request coming from the man who had experienced Christ's presence on the Damascus Road, who had been taught by the Lord in the desert for three years, who had been caught up into the third heaven and had experienced such revelation that he wasn't even allowed to speak of it?

—Adapted from David Butts, *A Call to Prayer*

Praising God STARTER KIT

God's Qualities

wisdom ....*Proverbs 9:10*
creativity ....*Psalm 19:1–4*
protection..........*1 Peter 3:12, 13*

compassion ....*Psalm 103:13*
fairness.................*Matthew 5:45*
generosity.............*James 1:17*

God's Greatness and Authority

"Wealth and honor come from you; you are the ruler of all things. In your hands are strength and power to exalt and give strength to all" (1 Chronicles 29:12).

"How majestic is your name in all the earth!" (Psalm 8:1).

"Ascribe to the Lord glory and strength" (Psalm 29:1).

God's Throne

"Righteousness and justice are the foundation of your throne" (Psalm 89:14).

"He sits enthroned between the cherubim, let the earth shake" (Psalm 99:1).

"Who is like the Lord our God, the One who sits enthroned on high" (Psalm 113:5).

God's Unfailing Love

"Give thanks to the Lord, for his love endures forever" (2 Chronicles 20:21).

"But I trust in your unfailing love" (Psalm 13:5).

"Praise be to the Lord, for he showed his wonderful love to me" (Psalm 31:21).

Six

Prayer for the World

*T*he power of prayer was demonstrated by the events that developed in the former Soviet Union and Eastern Europe at the turn of the nineties decade. For approximately seventy years Christians around the world had prayed that the misleading and misguided forces of Communism would fall and that the gospel would be proclaimed openly there.

The results of this decades-old strategy of prayer were finally seen. It was not Gorbachev, Reagan, or Bush who brought down the Berlin Wall or the Iron Curtain. The collapse of Communism, once seemingly invincible, was a direct response to the fervent, righteous prayers of faithful men and women following Jesus' teaching and strategy to pray.

No matter what the issue, situation, or problem, prayer is the first and best strategy. It is the alpha and omega to the Christian's way of living. It is the ultimate, supreme strategy for our lost world. Prayer is the key weapon to our spiritual warfare.

—Adapted from Gary Barnes, *A Call to Prayer*

Central Theme: Christians desiring to obey the Great Commission but who do not go overseas can be "stateside missionaries" in their unflagging commitment to pray for the unreached.

Lesson Aim: Group members will consider the role of prayer in world missions and choose their own commitment to this role.

Bible Background: 1 Kings 18:16–39

For Further Study: Read Chapter Six, "The Ultimate Strategy," in *A Call to Prayer.*

PLAN ONE

Classes

**Materials
You'll Need
For This Session**

Resource Sheets 6A–6C,
pens or pencils, Trans-
parency 6A, small pieces
of paper, a container

BUILDING COMMUNITY

Distribute copies of Resource Sheet 6A and read aloud the story at the top of the page. Then present the problem: **What could you say to David if he feels he's not helping the efforts of world missions?** Ask class members to read the information on the sheet and choose the item they think would be most helpful to use in encouraging David.

When class members are ready with ideas, seat yourself in front of the class and say that you're going to act as if you're David, waiting for encouragement. Try to get class members to do more than read what is on the sheet, but to retell it in a way that is helpful to others.

When they're finished, mention any stories, quotes, or facts they've left out.

Case Study
10 Minutes

Distribute copies of Resource Sheet 6A and read aloud the story at the top of the page. **State that missions often seem like an all-or-nothing proposition. Either we're obeying the Great Commission and going overseas or we're staying home and doing nothing.** (For anyone who is unfamiliar with the Great Commission, read Matthew 28:19, 20.) **Ask class members to choose from these categories:**

1. I never feel like a missionary (one who works in cross-cultural evangelism).
2. I sometimes feel like a missionary.
3. I frequently feel like a missionary.

Then take turns reading the rest of the material on Resource Sheet 6A and ask a few class members to tell which item is most meaningful to them.

OPTION
Survey
5–7 Minutes

CONSIDERING SCRIPTURE

Ask class members to turn to 1 Kings 18 and assign the following parts to willing class members.
- Ahab: v. 17
- Elijah: vv. 18, 19, 21, 22–24, 25, 27, 30, 33, 34, 36, 37
- Prophet of Baal: v. 26
- The people: vv. 24, 39

Dramatic Reading
15 Minutes

Write the above lists for each character on the chalkboard or on a sheet of paper. The narrator reads everything else—you may wish to do this or to assign it to someone familiar with reading the Bible aloud.

After the narrator and "actors" have read the passage, ask "Elijah" to reread verses 36 and 37. Ask class members, **What are the elements in this prayer?** After they answer, summarize with these three elements:
- The people would know that God is truly God.
- The people would know Elijah was his obedient servant.
- The people would turn to him.

Ask, **If we were to use these same elements in a missionary prayer, what would that prayer be?**

Distribute small pieces of paper and pencils and have class members read 1 Kings 18:16–39 silently. **Ask them to write one question about the facts or meaning of the passage.** They should also write their initials. Collect these questions and put them in a container. Pass the container around and ask class members to draw out a question. After they've done so, move from person to person asking them to try to answer the question. If they're confused by the question, they can check the initials and ask the writer of the question what they intended.

If you have more than nine class members, you may wish to assign members one of three sections from which their question should be drawn: vv. 16–21, 22–29, 30–39. Assign one extra person to vv. 36, 37, Elijah's prayer.

Read and React
10–15 minutes

Distribute copies of Resource Sheet 6B and ask three volunteers to read the three different paragraphs. After the first paragraph is read, display Transparency 6A. **Explain that each of these peoples lives apart from the others. They have different cultures, different geographical locations they call home, and often different languages. They don't communicate much with each other, and so a missionary from a neighboring tribe or from overseas needs to penetrate each people group.**

Let this visual remain on the overhead projector until the class dismisses.

TAKING THE NEXT STEP

Clear the chalkboard and write the numbers 1–10 vertically. **Challenge class members to come up with ten different ways, methods, or aids to pray for missions.** Encourage them to use any of the Resource Sheets you've provided.

Brainstorming
10 Minutes

Add any of these ideas when they're finished.
- Subscribe to *Global Prayer Digest* to help you remain interested in praying every day (GPD, US Center for World Mission, 1605 Elizabeth Street, Pasadena, CA 91104).
- Pray for a different continent every day of the week. Replace Antarctica by dividing Asia into two days: inland Asia and the Pacific nations.
- Explore the idea of sponsoring a Concert of Prayer. (The format is provided in *A Call to Prayer.*)
- Join (or start) a missions committee and organize a prayer strategy there.

Ask class members to choose a task they do daily and use that time to pray for world missions, especially unreached peoples. For example, they could pray for world missions every morning when they start their car or prepare coffee, or every evening when they set their alarm.

OPTION
Daily Reminder
3–5 Minutes

Close in prayer, asking God to help class members pray for missionaries. Then pray, according to 1 Kings 18:36, 37, that unreached peoples will know that God is God, turn their hearts to him, and realize the missionary is God's obedient servant.

Prayer Time
3 Minutes

PLAN TWO  **Groups**

BUILDING COMMUNITY

1. When you think of missions, who do you think of? A famous missionary? A missionary you've heard speak? A person at your church who talks about missions?

2. What do you think it means to be a "Great Commission Christian"?

3. OPTION: **Have you ever thought of serving as a missionary (taking the gospel to another culture)? If so, where?**

4. OPTION: **What would you say to someone who suggested that missionaries are the only "Great Commission Christians," meaning they're the only ones obeying the Great Commission?** (Read the Great Commission—Matthew 28:18–20—for anyone who is unfamiliar with it.)

CONSIDERING SCRIPTURE

Read *1 Kings 18:16–21.*

1. How did Elijah challenge the people of Israel and what was their response?

Read *1 Kings 18:22–29.*

2. What preparations did the prophets of Baal make?

3. **Why do you think Elijah taunted the prophets of Baal?** (The high drama of this scene and his taunts were probably to create an event Israel would never forget so that they would be more motivated to obey God.)

Read *1 Kings 18:30–39.*

4. What extra measures did Elijah use to insure that the fire was a miracle?

> **Materials You'll Need For This Session**
>
> Resource Sheets 6A, 6B; pencils; small pieces of paper or index cards

Accountability Partners

Have partners meet and discuss their progress in praying for world missions. If they chose a time to pray and it isn't working out, encourage them to choose another. It might also be helpful if they brought their handouts to the meeting to review.

Worship Ideas

• Read Psalm 67 together as an act of worship, noting the number of times the words "peoples" and "nations" occur.

• Song Suggestions: "Raise Up an Army, O God," by Steve and Vikki Cook; "Shine, Jesus, Shine," by Graham Kendrick; "We've a Story to Tell to the Nations," by H. Ernest Nichol

Memory Verse

"He told them, 'The harvest is plentiful, but the workers are few. Ask the Lord of the harvest, therefore, to send out workers into his harvest field'" (Luke 10:2).

---

5. How did the fire respond to Elijah's extra measures?

6. What was the response of the people?

7. What specific things was Elijah praying for God to do in verses 36 and 37?

TAKING THE NEXT STEP

1. Distribute pieces of paper or index cards, and ask group members to write a prayer about missions based on 1 Kings 18:36, 37.

2. Distribute copies of <u>Resource Sheet 6B</u>.

• **Which of these facts surprise you, if any?**

• **What specific requests about missions can we pray for, based on this handout?**

3. Distribute copies of <u>Resource Sheet 6A</u> and ask someone to read the true stories.

• **Do any of the true stories give you ideas about how you can be a better prayer supporter of world missions?**

• **Is there a time every day that you would like to commit to praying for world missions?**

IS PRAYER **REAL** MISSIONARY WORK?

Two friends felt a call to fulfill the Great Commission through missionary work. Ron went overseas and worked with a tribe of people that had heard little about Jesus Christ. David remained at home and got a job and raised a family. Everyday, however, David prayed for the people Ron was trying to reach. He prayed for Ron's welfare. When Ron wrote David with his prayer requests, David prayed for him faithfully.

Years later, David confesses to you that he feels guilty because he is not doing missionary work.

WHAT WILL YOU SAY?

The lie of the enemy is that prayer is not important missionary work and that praying for missionaries is second-class missions work. Which of the items below would you like to use to encourage David?

1. QUOTE: "World evangelization, above all, is an issue to be decided by spiritual power, the power of the Holy Spirit released in response to the prayers of his people."
—*John D. Robb*

2. TRUE STORY: Missionary Stan Yoder tells a story about when he worked in Sierra Leone. He wanted to reach the Yalunka people there, so he and his agency targeted a Yalunka town, and the agency was recruiting a couple to come work there. About the same time, a church in the U.S. began praying for the Yalunka town, praying specifically that twelve families would come to Christ. Before the couple came, the following happened. A new chief was elected, and he sent word to Stan to come and start a church there. Stan went, and 250 people attended the first service, and 21 people came to Christ the first day.   —*From author's interview with Stan Yoder*

3. TRUE STORY: Since the 1800s missionaries have tried to reach the 20,000 semi-nomadic Orma people of Kenya. This people was highlighted in July 1986 in the daily missions prayer devotional, *Global Prayer Digest.* After the article was printed, it worked out that nine missionaries were able to come among the Ormas.
—*From* Mission Frontiers, *"We Pray, God Answers" March 1989*

4. FACT: Prayer is mentioned more than thirty times in the book of Acts, generally before major breakthroughs in the outward expansion of the early Christian movement.

5. TRUE STORY: Dick Eastman, president of World Literature Crusade, tells how in 1988 God led him to take a team of pray-ers throughout Eastern Europe. In obedience to God's leading, they carried out a "prayer walk" around the Politbureau building in Bucharest, where less than two years later Ceaucescu made his last stand after pridefully announcing his regime would last a thousand years.

UPDATE ON *Missions*

[Jesus] told them, "The harvest is plentiful, but the workers are few. Ask the Lord of the harvest, therefore, to send out workers into his harvest field" (Luke 10:2).

THE CHALLENGE: *The harvest is plentiful.*

Jesus said nearly two thousand years ago that the harvest was plentiful. The challenge is still before us today. Over 3.5 billion people on our planet do not know Jesus Christ and God's gift of grace and forgiveness. These people are part of 12,000 unreached people groups from around the world. These peoples, according to the Adopt A People Clearinghouse, are deemed "unreached" for three reasons:

✦ They have not had the gospel preached to them.
✦ They do not have a church in their language or culture.
✦ They do not have the Word of God translated into their language.

These groups make up more than 65 percent of our earth's population.

THE PROBLEM: *The workers are few.*

The laborers are few, as these statistics show:

✦ More than 50 percent of the new missionary workers who go to the field will stay an average of only one four-year term.
✦ More than 80 percent of the present missionary force will work with "reached" groups; that is, they have a significant population claiming to be Christian with leaders who are nationals.
✦ Less than 18 percent of the present missionary force work in the fifty-five least evangelized countries of the world (more than 3 billion population).
✦ More than 50 percent of the present missionary force working around the world will reach retirement age or die over the next ten years.
✦ The average U.S. congregation gives only 2.5 percent of its budget to missions.

THE ANSWER: *Ask the Lord of the harvest.*

We do not need more committees, more satellites, more colleges, or more books on missions and evangelism. We do not need more seminars, workshops, conventions, or conferences. Instead, Jesus calls people to take seriously the ministry of prayer. Jesus yearns for more prayer warriors and prayer meetings. He aches for more meetings opened in prayer, focused on prayer, and concluded with prayer!

—Adapted from Gary Barnes, *A Call to Prayer*

THE TARGET:

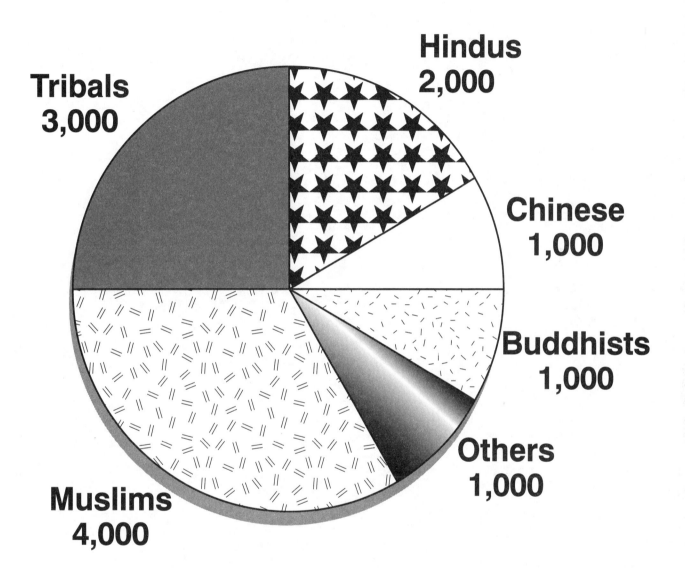

Tribals 3,000

Hindus 2,000

Chinese 1,000

Buddhists 1,000

Others 1,000

Muslims 4,000

12,000
UNREACHED PEOPLES

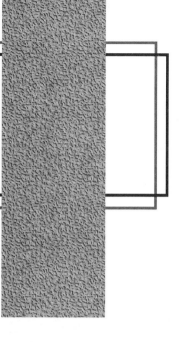

Seven

Praying With Others

*P*rayer can be solitary or communal, private or public, spontaneous or studied. I have found regular prayer times with a few close friends to be extremely helpful in deepening my prayer life. Jesus said, "Where two or three come together in my name, there am I with them" (Matthew 18:20).

Like an orator who becomes enamored with the sound of his own voice and struts his eloquence in order to call attention to his superior mastery of words, we can, if we are not careful, become more excited about prayer than about the God with whom we communicate through our prayers.

The focus on prayer can be so easily blurred. We need clarity of mind and spirit if we are to pray as we ought. It is very easy to make prayer the end in itself rather than seeing it as a means to the end of knowing and pleasing God.

—Adapted from Ward Patterson, *A Call to Prayer*

Central Theme: Praying with others can give us confidence and increase our faith.

Lesson Aim: Group members will examine how Jesus prayed with others and explore the possibilities of praying with others more effectively.

Bible Background: Mark 14:32–41

For Further Study: Read Chapter Eight, "Deepening Your Prayer Life," in *A Call to Prayer.*

Materials You'll Need For This Session

Resource Sheets 7A and 7B, pens or pencils, Transparency 7A, chalkboard and chalk

PLAN ONE

Classes

BUILDING COMMUNITY

Display Transparency 7A and cover the lower portion. Pose the first question at the top of the transparency. **Ask class members to respond according to one of the faces printed below the question.** Encourage them to be honest. If they think praying with others is boring, they should say so. **Then pose the second question and ask for responses. Write the number of class members' responses under each face.**

Plan to make three lists on the chalkboard. Challenge class members to:

1. Try to list at least ten different occasions in which we pray with someone else. Use the following to spur discussion, if necessary.
- praying with our children
- praying when visiting someone in the hospital
- gathering before church services to pray for attendees and the service
- praying together with other Sunday school or VBS workers
- sharing a meal with friends
- studying the Bible together
- meeting someone for breakfast and praying together afterward

2. Try to list at least ten reasons to pray together.
- a good way to learn to pray
- can feel more confident because several of you are agreeing on something
- can bounce your prayer off someone else to see if it makes sense to them

3. Try to list at least ten ways praying with one or more other people can go wrong.
- someone may go on and on and become boring (guaranteed way to kill a prayer meeting)
- someone may use big words to try to impress us
- someone may pray about things I don't know about and am not involved in
- someone may get preachy
- my mind wanders

Opinions
5–7 Minutes

OPTION
Brainstorming
10 Minutes

CONSIDERING SCRIPTURE

Letter Writing
10–15 Minutes

Distribute copies of Resource Sheet 7A and have class members read ***Mark 14:32–41*** silently. Then give these instructions: **Write a letter as if you were Peter, James, or John, and address it to your wife. Be sure to tell what happened in the passage. Also, be sure to include what you think Jesus meant by "keep watch."**

Allow class members about ten minutes to do this. Circulate among them to see if anyone is stumped. After the allotted time, ask volunteers to read their letters.

Point out how troubled Jesus was in verse 33 and how fervently he asked them to stay with him in verse 34.

OPTION
Monologue
10–15 Minutes

If some of your class members are better at talking than writing, encourage them to read the passage silently and consider how they as Peter, James, or John would have expressed this out loud. **Then put them up front with an empty chair next to them and ask them to present how they think that apostle reacted.** Their monologue should include the events of the passage and what the class member thinks it means to "keep watch."

OPTION
Checking Cross References
5 Minutes

What does it mean to "keep watch"?
Have someone read ***Mark 13:34, 35 and Acts 20:28,*** and then ask volunteers to tell what they think this phrase means. (The first reference seems to refer to being attentive to world events and what they mean. The second refers to monitoring our own behavior and the behavior of others as overseers. From these passages, the phrase seems to mean to "be attentive.")

Ask, **What might we learn if we stay attentive to God during group prayer?** (God might give us ideas, impressions from what others say. God may convict us of our own attitude as another speaks.)

TAKING THE NEXT STEP

Distribute copies of <u>Resource Sheet 7B</u> and read it aloud for the class.

Ask class members to come up with group guidelines for praying together based on what the class has read, studied, and discussed. (If you didn't do the first brainstorming session at the beginning, mention now the various occasions in which praying together can occur.)

After suggestions have been made, bring up any of these issues that aren't mentioned.

- Choose a focus—too many topics can be confusing.
- Mention only shared concerns unless you explain beforehand what you're talking about.
- Be as specific as possible.
- Say it, spit it out, don't go on and on.
- Be honest—be willing to tell God you don't know what to ask for.
- Don't pretend to be interested in things you aren't interested in.
- When your mind wanders, try to "keep watch" and stay attentive to what God might be saying to you through the prayers of another.

Invite class members to offer a sentence prayer, asking God to help their prayer life grow in some way.

Forming Guidelines
10–15 Minutes

Prayer Time
5 Minutes

PLAN TWO  **Groups**

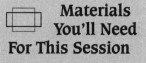
Materials You'll Need For This Session

Transparency 7A

BUILDING COMMUNITY

Distribute copies of <u>Transparency 7A</u> and tell group members to look at the bottom portion. Ask them to mark where on each continuum they fall and then to share that with the rest of the group. Then ask the following questions.

1. Why do Christians think it's a good idea to pray together?

2. Why do some people dislike praying together?

3. OPTION: **Tell about a good experience you've had praying with another person (that doesn't mean you prayed aloud).**

4. OPTION: **Why bother praying together? Isn't it good enough to pray by ourselves?**

CONSIDERING SCRIPTURE

Read *Mark 14:32–41.*

1. Have you ever had someone say to you, "Sit here while I pray"? What do you think about Jesus saying that to the apostles?

2. How do you think Peter, James, and John felt about being singled out?

3. How does it affect you that the Son of God asked his friends to be with him while he prayed?

4. What do you think it means for us that he did this? (We don't need to be embarrassed that we need other people.)

5. If you have ever prayed on your knees or laying down with your face to the ground (as Jesus seems to have done in v. 35), tell how it felt to you.

OPTION

Accountability Partners

Have group members meet and discuss how this past session about praying together is significant to the accountability-partner relationship. What are they doing right? Do they need to make any changes?

OPTION

Worship Ideas

• Read Psalm 46 together as an act of worship.

• Song Suggestions: "As We Gather," by Tommy Coombs; "The Family of God," by Gloria and William Gaither; "We Gather Together," by Theodore Baker and E. Kremser

OPTION

Memory Verse

"'My soul is overwhelmed with sorrow to the point of death,' he said to them. 'Stay here and keep watch'" (Mark 14:34).

6. How do you think Peter, James, and John looked back on that evening (besides wishing they had stayed awake)?

7. If they had stayed awake, how might they have not fallen into temptation?

8. What do people do when they "keep watch"?

9. How can we stay attentive when others are praying?

10. When people have prayed together for a while, how do you think it affects their relationship?

TAKING THE NEXT STEP

1. Review the many topics these sessions have covered: believing in the power of prayer, praying in a down-to-earth way, removing the hindrances of prayer, fitting prayer into our daily pattern, using prayer to find intimacy with God, praying for world missions.

2. Ask group members to complete these sentences:

• **The most important fact or attitude I've learned from this class has been . . .**

• **As a result of this class, I need to . . .**

3. If your group is larger than ten, divide into two groups. Ask group members to offer a brief prayer, thanking God for the group and asking him to help them in one specific area of prayer.

Gethsemane Letter

Dear Mrs. _____,

As you know, Jesus is in the midst of a trial. They're trying to convict him of blasphemy. You will never believe what I did, though!

No longer worthy to be called an apostle,

Covenanting With Others in Prayer

WHEN I WAS at the University of Indiana, we in the speech department developed a small prayer group. We established a closeness with one another and with God that was a strength to us in the daily demands of our studies.

In my campus ministry, I was in a prayer partnership with a fellow campus minister. We prayed together about our separate works, and I shared in his vision for a mission to Oxford, England, where he and his wife now serve.

In my teaching ministry, I look forward to my weekly prayer time with two fellow faculty members. Their faith and consistency in Christ have helped me to go deeper in my walk with him.

Wherever we may be, there is someone else with whom we can enter into a partnership of regular prayer. If you have not found such a person or persons, you may want to pray that God will lead you to an appropriate partnership of prayer.

—Ward Patterson, *A Call to Prayer*

How Do You Feel About . . .

1. praying with one other person (you don't have to pray aloud)?

2. praying with a whole group (you don't have to pray aloud)?

CONFIDENT

INTERESTED

INDIFFERENT

BORED

HORRIFIED

OBSTINATE

❖   ❖   ❖   ❖   ❖   ❖

I like praying ————————————|———————— I don't like praying
with others.   with others.

Group praying is ———————————|———————— Group praying is
interesting.   boring.

Asking Good Questions

NOTHING GLUES A LESSON TOGETHER and delivers the punch as well as good questions. Jesus himself asked more questions than he answered. Asking questions not only helps students retain information, it lets them experience the thrill of discovering truth for themselves.

FOUR KINDS OF QUESTIONS

Warm-up questions help us pull students out of the hurry of the day and focus on the lesson topic. They ask students to identify feelings, opinions, or situations in their lives:

- Why is it so hard to wait for problems to work out?
- When have you seen someone express hope? (You may use a real person or a character from a book, movie, or comic strip.)
- When has it looked to you as if God wasn't working against an unjust cause?

Test the question by imagining that you've just dressed three kids, fed them breakfast, and ridden in the car with them for ten minutes. Ask yourself the warm-up question again. Did it force you to think too much too fast or did it entice you?

Information questions ask participants to look for facts relevant to the study's theme:

- What happened in this passage to upset the Pharisees?
- Which words in this passage point to God's majesty?
- What does this passage say about how a pure person should and shouldn't behave?

Clarifying questions challenge participants to compare facts in the passage with facts they already know, to look in the context for clues:

- How does Judas' behavior in this passage (when he betrayed Christ) compare to Peter's behavior after he denied Christ?
- Based on the context, what does the phrase, "gentle and quiet spirit" appear to mean?

Teachers often compose these questions by thinking of how the text could be misunderstood: How do you reconcile the command to confess sins to one another (James 5:16) with the fact that Christ is the only mediator between God and man (1 Timothy 2:5)?

Application questions connect the facts of the lesson with moments in life when these facts could make a difference. You might begin with general questions, such as, "How do most people show favoritism?" Then ask them to identify situations in their own lives:

- When in your life have you felt the way Paul did in Romans 7:14-20?
- Describe a "Red Sea experience" in which you believe God helped you.
- What would you say to someone who doubted God as Thomas did?

Try to word these questions so they ask for constructive suggestions: "Think of situations in which you've been generous and tell why it didn't seem too difficult," rather than berating ourselves, "Why aren't we as generous as we should be?"

Even with application questions, have answers ready to suggest after participants have answered or to prime the pump for a class that is stumped. This means we have to know something about the students' lives so we can think of situations in which the lesson facts could make a difference.

HINTS FOR ASKING GOOD QUESTIONS

Why Ask Why? Because questions are designed to draw people out, avoid asking questions that require a yes or no answer. If you must ask one, follow up with "Why?" or "Why not?" Instead of asking vague questions such as, "What is the application of this passage?" be specific and ask "What does this passage tell us about our relationships with other people?" After you formulate a question, answer it yourself. Was it too difficult to answer? Did you use facts your students will not know? If so, restate the question.

The Sound of Silence. Don't be afraid of silence after you ask a question. If the question was insightful, students will have to consider it for a few moments. The best advice I was ever given about asking questions was to wait until I had counted to twenty-five silently before jumping in to rephrase it.

Most classes have two or three people who don't participate in a discussion. If you think it's appropriate, ask that quiet, thoughtful child or adult: "Dennis, how do you feel about this? I'd like to hear your ideas."

Quieter students find it easier to talk if given graduated, multiple choice answers. To the question, "How would you have felt if you had been in the rich young ruler's shoes?" offer these possibilities: not upset, mildly upset, very upset. With excessively quiet students, try asking students to tell their answers to the person next to them first; then, ask everyone to report that same answer to a small group or the class. This gives shy or quiet students a chance to think about and rehearse their answer on another person before attempting to report to the group.

Before asking a question that requires participants to be vulnerable, you might confess one of your own shortcomings: "I yelled at my kids this week when they spilled bleach on the carpet. What makes you angry?" On the other hand, don't focus only on digging up dirt. Ask students to report their progress too: "When do you find it easiest to praise God?" "What improvement have you seen in your attitudes about money over the years?" Discussing how God has worked in our lives helps students spur one another on to love and good works.

—Jan Johnson

Promote Your Class or Group!

Get People's Attention With This Ready-to Use Clip Art.

Copy the art from these pages to use in your church newsletters or bulletins. Make your own creative posters to grab people's attention. Use the ready-made handouts as bulletin inserts or flyers. Make up letters or post cards to send to past and present attendees, friends, and others you'd like to invite. Be creative and get the message out, and then prepare with prayer to lead all the people you reach!

Have you ever wanted to learn how to pray . . .

✧ more effectively?
✧ more sincerely?
✧ with more power?
✧ without hindrances?

Many people desire to pray but feel they lack the practical knowledge to be true men and women of prayer. This class will give the practical help you need to become a prayer warrior, one whom God can use to change the world.

A Call to Prayer

Dates: _____

Time: _____

Location: _____

For Information, Call: _____

OTHER CREATIVE GROUPS GUIDES
from Standard Publishing

FIND US FAITHFUL

Guide by Mike McCann
Learn from the examples in Scripture how to pass the faith along to the next generation. All Christians need to communicate their faith to others. For Christian parents, that responsibility is multiplied. Thirteen sessions will help assure that all who come behind us will find us faithful.
Order number 11-40308 *(ISBN 0-7847-0308-6)*

CLAIMING YOUR PLACE

Guide by Michael C. Mack and Mark A. Taylor
Help your small group or class learn how they can find where they fit into the life of the church. Seven sessions will guide your group to greater commitment and involvement in the body. They'll find a place of faith, service, bold witness, passion, flexibility, and more.
Order number 11-40305 *(ISBN 0-7847-0285-3)*

HEARING GOD

Guide by Michael C. Mack and Mark A. Taylor
Help your group or class learn how to read God's Word—and really understand it! In just six lessons, you will demonstrate eight simple steps that can make anyone feel at home in the Bible and be able to put it into practice.
Order number 11-40306 *(ISBN 0-7847-0286-1)*

To order, contact your local Christian bookstore.
(If the book is out of stock, you can order by calling 1-800-543-1353.)

STANDARD
PUBLISHING
Cincinnati, Ohio

To purchase a copy of
A Call to Prayer,
contact your local
Christian bookstore.

(If the book is out of stock, you can order
by calling 1-800-543-1353.)

11-03011 *(ISBN 0-87403-999-1)*